presented to:

from:

THE *Twenty-Third Psalm* *for the* Single Parent

To: Lorie
love: Tanya
:)

Happy Mother's Day!

THE TWENTY-THIRD *Psalm*

-*for the*-
Single Parent

CARMEN LEAL

The Twenty-Third Psalm for the Single Parent

Published by AMG Publishers, an imprint of Living Ink Books
6815 Shallowford Rd.
Chattanooga, Tennessee 37421

ISBN 0-89957-175-1
First printing—September 2005

Cover designed by Market Street Design, Inc., Chattanooga, Tennessee
Interior design and typesetting by The Livingstone Corporation, Carol Stream, Illinois
Edited and proofread by Agnes Lawless, Dan Penwell, The Livingstone Corporation, Sharon Neal, and Rick Steele.

Printed in Italy

11 10 09 08 07 06 05- L -8 7 6 5 4 3 2 1

To Nicholas and Justin,
the best sons a single
mother ever had.
With the Shepherd's help,
you turned out to be
special men of character.
I love and appreciate you
more than words can express.
See you on *Oprah*, Justin.

Contents

Introduction

Mountain-Moving Faith

You know you're in trouble when not one but two people approach you at church on the same Sunday and give you a copy of *The Strong-Willed Child* by James Dobson. I fumed as I drove home from church a few weeks after my husband moved out, the unsolicited books condemning me from the passenger seat. I'd always thought of my sons as rambunctious, or maybe high-spirited, but strong willed? Nicholas and Justin are just angry about the divorce, I justified. They'll calm down when we have a routine.

I tell you the truth, if you have faith as small as a mustard seed, you can say to this mountain, "Move from here to there" and it will move. Nothing will be impossible for you.
—Matthew 17:20

But the seeds of doubt had been planted, and I began to worry that maybe I wasn't the best parent to have custody of my two elementary school-age boys. If they were a challenge now, what would happen when they became teenagers?

Neither of us were Christians when we had

met, but five years into the marriage I gave my life to Christ. I then fell into the same trap as other wives who try to trick their husbands into becoming Christians—tracts scattered around the house, Bibles open to specific passages, Christian stations programmed on every dial of the car radio. No matter what I did, and I now understand I couldn't do anything to make him a Christian, he resisted. In fact, the closer I drew to the Shepherd, the harder my husband's heart grew. Now here I was, a single mom caught in what was going to be a long, bitter custody battle.

The next week I hung up from a heated phone conversation with their dad about who had messed up the visitation schedule, only to break up a fight between my children. I couldn't do this for the year to eighteen months that my attorney had predicted the divorce and custody battle might take. Worse, I didn't think my children could take it.

Instead of praying like I knew I should, I cried and worried. I never doubted that my husband loved his sons, but I felt that the children should live with me. We'd both made huge mistakes in our marriage, words and actions that could never be undone, but now we had to do what was best for Nicholas and Justin. With more than a little relief, I waved them off for their weekend with Dad.

On Sunday I came late to church, avoiding the marriage and single-adult classes that were not appropriate for a newly separated woman. The parenting group was another place I avoided. How could I ever raise kids God's way when I couldn't keep my marriage together? I walked into the sanctuary hopeless about getting through the next hour without crying, let alone through the next ten years of single parenting. On this Sunday, however, the Shepherd, knowing I faced what felt like an impossible situation, had the perfect message for me.

That day the pastor told the story of a small congregation that had built a new sanctuary on a piece of land willed to them by a church member. Ten days before their first service, the local building inspector dropped a bomb: An ordinance required more parking spaces for the larger building. Until the parking lot was doubled in size, the new sanctuary was off-limits.

Faith moves mountains, but you have to keep pushing while you are praying.
—Mason Cooley

It was not a matter of money, which would have been bad enough since the church members had used all their resources on the new building, but the only land left was the mountain against which the church had been built.

"We'll just have to move the mountain," explained the pastor to his flock the next Sunday morning. The congregation's skeptical responses didn't faze the pastor. Undaunted, he announced that he would meet that evening with any members who had "mountain-moving faith." All they had to do was to pray for God to move the mountain from their backyard and provide them with enough money to have the land paved and painted before the scheduled dedication service—in exactly one week.

That night twenty-four of the three hundred members gathered for a congregational prayer session. They didn't point fingers at the contractor who had not known about the parking-lot law. They didn't bicker about how to make the impossible happen. Instead, they prayed for three hours about a seemingly impossible situation.

"We'll open next Sunday as scheduled," the pastor said after the last "amen." He assured those with mountain-moving faith that the Shepherd had not brought them this far to let them down.

The next morning, a rough-looking construction foreman came, hardhat in hand, to the pastor's study asking a favor. "We're building a new shopping mall in the next county over," he explained. "We need some landfill, and that mountain behind the church is perfect. If you'd be willing to sell us a piece and if we can have it right away, we'll pay you for the dirt and pave the level area free of charge."

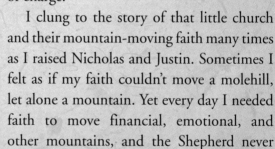

I clung to the story of that little church and their mountain-moving faith many times as I raised Nicholas and Justin. Sometimes I felt as if my faith couldn't move a molehill, let alone a mountain. Yet every day I needed faith to move financial, emotional, and other mountains, and the Shepherd never let me down. With prayer He guided me through custody, homework, moving, and the Dreaded *D*s—discipline, driving, and dating.

Sir Edmund Hillary, the first man to climb Mt. Everest, said, "It is not the mountain we conquer but ourselves." When I felt as if I were going through the "valley of the shadow of death" the Shepherd helped me conquer my frustrations, fears, and loneliness. In every area of my life as a single parent, the Shepherd answered my prayers.

The Twenty-Third Psalm for Single Parents is filled with stories of imperfect, hurting people, some of us with strong-willed children, who, through the Shepherd, found wholeness and happiness. Whether your faith is below sea level or you're ready to scale the Alps, the Lord is your Shepherd, and He will provide. All you need is mountain-moving faith.

The LORD is my shepherd, I shall not be in want.
He makes me lie down in green pastures,
he leads me beside quiet waters, he restores my soul.
He guides me in paths of righteousness for his name's sake.
Even though I walk through the valley of the shadow of death,
I will fear no evil, for you are with me;
your rod and your staff, they comfort me.
You prepare a table before me in the presence of my enemies.
You anoint my head with oil; my cup overflows.
Surely goodness and love will follow me all the days of my life,
and I will dwell in the house of the LORD forever.

PSALM 23

CHAPTER ONE

THE SHEPHERD WHO *Cares*

"THE LORD IS MY SHEPHERD"

SOMEONE CARES

It wasn't only his good looks that drew Christina to Merrill, though he was a handsome man with his long-lashed brown eyes and infectious grin punctuated by flashing dimples. But it was more than the packaging that caught Christina's attention when the two met at Bible college in 1979.

Even at such a young age, Merrill seemed the sort of man who would do great things for God. Gentle of spirit and possessing an incredible singing voice, Merrill was intelligent, sincere, and, like Christina, had a passion to serve God. They married in 1984 and grew deeper in love with each passing year. She was his queen, and he treated her

O LORD, you are my God; I will exalt you and praise your name, for in perfect faithfulness you have done marvelous things, things planned long ago.
—Isaiah 25:1

like royalty. Together they served in the ministry, first with Merrill as a youth pastor and eventually as the senior pastor of the church they started.

David was born in 1990. They longed for more children, but throughout 1992, nagging fatigue plagued Merrill. Then in the spring of 1993, the couple attended an out-of-state pastors' conference. Their first night home, Merrill couldn't sleep.

"Honey, something's wrong." The pressure in Merrill's chest frightened him.

"What do you mean?"

"It's my heart."

"Merrill, I can actually see your heart beating fast in your chest. We need to get to the hospital. Now!"

"I think my husband is having a heart attack," explained a frantic Christina to the admitting clerk after racing to the hospital.

The erratic EKG results triggered the need for

further tests. Drawing blood is a routine procedure, but no matter how many times the nurse tried, she couldn't fill even one vial. A healthy male has a hemoglobin count of between fourteen and seventeen, but when Merrill was admitted to the hospital, they discovered his was under five. He was losing blood, and they didn't know why. Something was terribly wrong.

Eventually, Merrill was diagnosed with primary sclerosing cholangitis, a rare liver disease. For the next five and one-half years, he was in and out of hospitals, yet he continued in ministry.

"He never complained," says Christina who remembers the blood transfusions and procedures. "No matter how tired he was and regardless of the pain, Merrill studied, preached, sang, counseled, and did everything God asked him to do."

In December 1997, Merrill entered the hospital for the last time.

"Please heal him, Lord. I don't want to be a widow," prayed Christina to the Shepherd as she sat near her beloved husband. But on January 8, 1998, Merrill finished his extraordinary race.

Now Christina faced many decisions. Should she get a job? Sell the house? Keep David in private school? With the help of family, friends, and a mother-in-law who loved her like a daughter, Christina made life-changing decisions for herself and her son. She wallowed in her loneliness, crying more tears than she thought a human body could hold. How could she survive without such a caring husband in her life? Together Christina and David grieved for the man who was everything to them.

In June 1999, the little family decided to relocate to Colorado Springs where Merrill had been an associate pastor. They had maintained friendships, and it felt like the right move. Christina sold the house and, with the help of several friends, packed the furniture and their belongings. With hearts full of hope for the future, they began their new lives.

They found a church and reconnected with old friends and made new ones. Christina found a job, and David started school. Life began to fall into a cycle.

"The most important thing in my life was David," says Christina. "When you are the only parent, everything falls on you. Watching your son grieve is the most painful experience possible. You'd give anything to take away his loss, to take away your loss, to give him back his father. But all you can do is be Mom. You can't be Dad.

"It was an incredibly lonely time," explains Christina about the first few years of being a single parent. "I worked, cooked, cleaned, went to church, did what I had to for David, and fell into bed at night, lonelier than the day before. I was in a survival mode."

One day in December 2003, Christina watched a jewelry commercial on television. *I don't have anyone to give me jewelry*, she thought watching a man slip the perfect diamond onto a woman's finger. She didn't want an engagement ring, for she wasn't even dating anyone, but she wanted someone to care for her.

"How far that little candle throws his beams! So shines a good deed in a weary world."
—William Shakespeare

The weeks leading to the annual church party were filled with work, decorating the house, and choosing gifts for David. Despite the holiday music and decorations, Christina's nagging sadness continued to grow each time she saw a jewelry commercial.

One night Christina prayed to the Shepherd that this would be a special Christmas for her.

They give away so many gifts at the church party, Lord. I've never won anything before. Could You give me something this year?

That evening Christina enjoyed the holiday music and food, but all the while hoped that the Shepherd would answer her prayer. Maybe it was silly, but now, five years since Merrill's last Christmas with her, she wanted to win something beautiful.

Though she had prayed for this moment, Christina was surprised when they called her name along with two other people from her table. As her friends clapped and yelled their delight, Christina walked to where the gifts were displayed.

She reached into the bowl and drew a ticket with the printed number showing which prize had been won. Each year a committee puts together a lavish display of televisions, CD players, trips, restaurant gift certificates, and other popular items. She held her breath and surveyed the wonderful choices. Any other year she would have been pleased to receive anything, but this time she wanted something that showed someone cared.

"That's mine!" screamed Christina when she heard her number announced. The only thing brighter than the unshed tears sparkling in Christina's eyes that evening were the diamonds in the jewelry presented to her.

When people realized what Christina had won, they began to cheer and Christina looked at her friends' beaming faces. The Shepherd had given her a gift that showed he truly did care enough to give her diamonds.

"It was as if the prize was meant for me," Christina says. "People came running to see what I had won. I felt so special."

She was amazed that this particular gift was even included in the mix.

"Although many of the items are duplicates, this was the only one of its kind," she said. "The gifts don't usually include jewelry, but this year one of the volunteers, a single mother, picked out a diamond ring and earring set and bought it with donated money. Only another single mother could know how much I wanted something frivolous. I'd never buy myself a diamond ring or earrings, yet the Shepherd gave them to me to show how much He cares."

When Christina admires the diamond on her finger and the sparkles on her ears, she thinks of the Shepherd who cared enough to send a reminder of His love.

God is a verb, not a noun proper or improper.
—R. Buckminster Fuller

A generous man will prosper;
he who refreshes others will himself be refreshed.
—Proverbs 11:25

PRAISE HIM, PRAISE HIM

FANNY CROSBY

Praise Him! Praise Him! Jesus, our blessed Redeemer!

Sing, O Earth, His wonderful love proclaim!

Hail Him! hail Him! highest archangels in glory;

Strength and honor give to His holy Name!

Like a shepherd, Jesus will guard His children,

In His arms He carries them all day long:

CHAPTER TWO

THE SHEPHERD WHO *Provides*

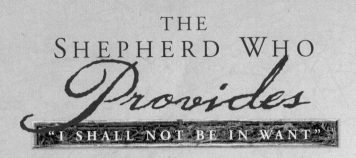

"I SHALL NOT BE IN WANT"

"SHEAR" SURVIVAL

Before either of my two younger sisters married, they shared a small house in Houston, Texas. Diane, a single mother, preferred housework, while Patricia agreed to take over the outdoor chores. At the time, Patricia worked and attended nursing school, usually arriving home when it was too dark to mow the lawn. Weekends were no better, and eventually, the grass grew out of control.

"Patricia, look at the yard," complained Diane. "The grass is up to my waist, and Mario can't even play outside. When are you going to cut it?"

"It's not that bad," Patricia argued.

For I am the LORD, your God, who takes hold of your right hand and says to you, Do not fear; I will help you.
—Isaiah 41:13

They walked into the backyard, and while the grass failed the waist-high test, it did touch their knees. Patricia, determining to raze the burgeoning grass before it grew even more unmanageable, took a day off and started mowing early in the morning.

She soon figured out she needed something more than their manual mower to do the job. The long grass twisted into the blades with each push. Hot and frustrated, Patricia wondered how to hack down the tropical rain forest of a yard.

She didn't have a sickle, a weed whacker, or anything even resembling a real garden tool. They probably didn't have the money to invest in a new mower, and the neighbors weren't home to lend a hand. Patricia finally called her sister at her office. "Diane, I can't do this anymore."

"Do what?"

"Cut the grass. It's too long, and my hands hurt."

"What do you mean your hands hurt? How can they hurt just from using the lawn mower?"

Patricia, on the verge of tears, looked at her hands. "The grass is too high and thick. The blades won't move anymore."

"So what are you using?"

"Scissors."

No, she couldn't have heard right. "Scissors!"

Patricia had used a pair of sewing scissors to cut the grass. Soon, blisters formed as the grips cut deeply into her flesh.

Diane burst out laughing. "I'm sorry, Patricia, but I've never heard of anyone cutting grass with a pair of scissors."

In her air-conditioned office, Diane laughed as Patricia, at home and drenched in sweat, cried.

"I'm going to have to stop," admitted Patricia

in defeat. "It's going to take a miracle to cut this grass."

Later, as Diane pulled into their driveway, she was still chuckling about cutting grass with a small pair of scissors. "Only Patricia," she laughed as she headed to the backyard.

Rounding the corner of the house, Diane stopped short.

"Patricia! Come out here. You're not going to believe this."

Running outside, Patricia stared first at Diane, then at the large animal in the backyard.

"Where did you get it?"

"I didn't get it. When I got home, it was here eating the grass."

The girls gleefully laughed at their "miracle"—a cow eating the grass that had been too high to mow. Somehow, the hungry cow had wandered through a broken fence and into their yard from a neighboring farm. Everyone was happy—the cow,

The first step in solving a problem is to tell someone about it.
—John Peter Flynn

Diane, and especially Patricia, who had needed a miracle.

Diane needed other miracles when she was on her own raising her son. When he was about nine years old, Mario played Little League baseball, but, between work and night school, she had a hard time with scheduling. She attended his games whenever possible, and to celebrate the end of the season one year, Diane promised Mario they'd eat at his favorite fast-food restaurant.

After the last game, Diane and Mario headed out for their victory dinner. Diane ordered their meal and drove to the window to pay.

"Oh no, I forgot to go to the bank," she said when she opened her nearly empty wallet. "I don't have enough money."

"But Mamma, you said we could eat here. I'm hungry."

Diane advanced to the pick-up window determined that Mario would get his celebration meal.

"Excuse me," she said to the attendant. "I didn't have time to get to the bank today. My son is hungry, so could I take the food and bring the money tomorrow?"

"Of course you can't!" replied the cashier. "You either give me the money, or you don't get the food."

"I promise I'll bring the money tomorrow after I go to the bank."

A line of cars filled with hungry customers formed behind Diane. Each time the employee told Diane she had to pay for the food, she begged him to trust her.

"Just leave, Mamma," said my embarrassed son.

"No, Mario. I promised you, and I'm not leaving without our food. I have the money, just not right now."

The line grew longer as Diane pleaded her case. Finally, willing to do anything to serve the waiting customers, the young man gave Diane the bag of food.

After work the next day, Diane got money from the bank and drove back to the restaurant. The same employee was manning the register.

"Here's your money," she said holding out a twenty-dollar bill.

"You didn't order anything yet," said the man.

"This is for yesterday. Remember me? I didn't have any money," Diane explained, "so you gave me our food, and I said I'd be back today."

"You came back? I don't believe you actually came back."

"Of course I did," said Diane. "I said I would, and here I am."

Maybe he wasn't used to people keeping their

promises, but the incredulous young man waved Diane away. "Just having you offer to pay is enough. Why don't you put the money in your son's piggy bank?"

Thanking the man, Diane drove off and later put the money in Mario's bank.

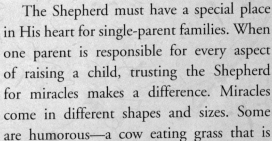

The Shepherd must have a special place in His heart for single-parent families. When one parent is responsible for every aspect of raising a child, trusting the Shepherd for miracles makes a difference. Miracles come in different shapes and sizes. Some are humorous—a cow eating grass that is too long to cut—and others are surprising, such as a person who bends the rules to help when one needs a break. Sometimes single parenting feels like cutting grass with a pair of scissors. The only way to survive is with a miracle from the Shepherd.

He gives strength to the weary and
increases the power of the weak.
—Isaiah 40:29

There are three stages in the work of God:
impossible, difficult, done.
—Hudson Taylor

NOW THANK WE ALL OUR GOD

MARTIN RINKART

Now thank we all our God, with heart and hands and voices,

Who wondrous things has done, in Whom this world rejoices;

Who from our mothers' arms has blessed us on our way

With countless gifts of love, and still is ours today.

CHAPTER THREE

THE SHEPHERD OF *Rest*

"HE MAKES ME LIE DOWN IN GREEN PASTURES"

WOODEN SPOONS

I reached for a wooden spoon to stir the soup and thought about the gift my son had given me years before. "Mom, you can open your present," Justin explained, "but only if you promise not to use it on me." The festive Christmas package, proudly yet childishly wrapped, did little to conceal the shape of the present so carefully chosen by my four-year-old.

Justin's eyes shone with excitement as he waited for the moment when I would unveil his treasure. "See, Mom, they're wooden spoons," he explained with great seriousness. "You need 'em to cook, but you gotta promise you won't spank me with 'em."

When the righteous cry for help, the LORD hears, and rescues them from all their troubles.
—Psalm 34:17

What happened to all those spoons? More important, what had happened to that little boy? I was still picturing the earnest expression as he offered me his gift—with strings attached—when I thought about the report card I had just opened. *I could break a dozen spoons on him and it wouldn't make a difference.*

Justin's high-school guidance counselor had called with yet another request for what I called our bimonthly tribunals. Over the last couple of years, teachers, counselors, and the principal asked to meet with me. He had failed almost every class and had no excuse. If I heard one more teacher say, "He's not working up to his potential," I'd whack them with something worse than a wooden spoon.

It wasn't just the grades, either. His continual anger at moving five thousand miles away from his father, his snotty attitude, and his unwillingness to interact with the family made him almost unbearable. He closeted himself upstairs in what I called his cave and talked on the phone to friends of questionable character and behavior. He dabbled with drugs and tobacco. He wasn't speaking to me, big surprise, because I had forbidden any interaction with his friend Peter. I'd even gone so far as to let Peter's mother know that Justin wasn't welcome at her home any longer.

"Mom, you insulted her!" screamed Justin when he heard my side of the conversation. "And it's not even true."

"Well, it's true as far as I can see. Peter *is* a prison sentence just waiting to happen, and he is not taking you with him as a cell mate." Maybe I could have phrased it better, but I didn't care that we were both single mothers and were supposed to help each other. I was tired and needed a rest. A few weeks after the phone call, Peter was arrested for drug possession, but I didn't feel like saying, "I told you so."

Now I had to follow through with my threat, no matter if it meant losing my son. At the start of the semester, Justin and I had talked about grades, goals, and general behavior. I'd tried making him go to church or youth group, but with his attitude, I knew he'd be disruptive enough that I'd get phone calls. I'd prayed, cried, whined, and everything I could think of, and now the only choice was whether he would take the morning or the afternoon flight. He was moving back to live with his father.

"Rest when you're weary. Refresh and renew yourself, your body, your mind, your spirit."
—Ralph Marston

I knew his father loved Justin, and he certainly was a better disciplinarian than I would ever be—wooden spoons or not. But he wasn't a Christian, and despite a ten-year cooling off period since the divorce, we still communicated best through lawyers. I had fought hard to win custody, and now I was sending my son back to the man I was convinced wasn't the better parent. I felt like a failure.

A few days later, I wiped away tears with the back of my hand as I drove home from the airport wondering how Justin would get along with his dad. *Keep my son safe*, I prayed to the Shepherd.

"Your son?" It wasn't an audible voice, but it was certainly the Shepherd. "Don't you know he's My son?"

At that point the vice squeezing my heart loosened a bit, and my breathing came easier. Of course, the Shepherd was right. As much as I loved my sons, the Shepherd had always loved them more. I had given my children to the Shepherd when they were little boys, and now I had to leave them in His trusting hands.

What will I do without Justin at home? Then I remembered I had asked for rest. I began to think about how much more restful it would be without the homework battles. I wouldn't have to cook nearly as much and wouldn't have the exhausting conflicts.

Justin spent his senior year in Hawaii with his dad. He somehow pulled together enough credits to graduate with a grade-point average significantly lower than his IQ warranted, but he did graduate. He didn't win any awards or go to the prom. He didn't send out invitations or get his class pictures. I would have forced him to do all those things, and, if the truth be told, I felt cheated out of his senior-year experience. But I did get a rest. I was able to pray for my son more than I had when he had lived with me, and the Shepherd answered those prayers.

Thanks to telephone calls and e-mail, Justin and I communicated more during his year away than we had during his previous three years combined. By living apart, I think Justin came to appreciate me in a new way. I certainly found a new appreciation for what a creative, loving, and handsome son the Shepherd had given to me.

I wish I could say that my son and his father became Christians that year, but it didn't happen. Justin did see firsthand some problems that caused our marriage to end, but he also saw how much his father loves him and how he is a blending of both parents.

The most important lesson I learned during that year of rest was that I was like the wooden spoons Justin had given me so many years before with one condition—I couldn't spank him with those particular spoons. Now I realize that, like the spoons, I'd loved Justin conditionally. I'd had a picture of the son he was capable of being, and that's the son I had wanted to love. But the Shepherd showed me that He has always loved me unconditionally, and now, after my year of rest, that's how I love Justin—with no strings attached.

The LORD replied, "My presence will go with you, and I will give you rest."
—Exodus 33:14

Sometimes the most urgent thing you can possibly do is take a complete rest.
—Ashleigh Brilliant

O THE DEEP, DEEP LOVE OF JESUS

Samuel T. Francis

O the deep, deep love of Jesus, love of every love the best!

'Tis an ocean full of blessing, 'tis a haven giving rest!

O the deep, deep love of Jesus, 'tis a heaven of heavens to me;

And it lifts me up to glory, for it lifts me up to Thee!

CHAPTER FOUR

THE SHEPHERD OF *Peace*

"HE LEADS ME BESIDE QUIET WATERS"

LOVE THE ONE YOU'RE WITH

Filled with optimism, Lori rushed into what she hoped was a marriage scripted by Disney. She just knew Clint was God's choice for a husband and that their love was strong enough to withstand any prejudice that might result from their biracial marriage. She had no idea of how to relate to the vast differences in their cultures, and being the wife of a United States marine was a new world for Lori. Still, she was confident that their love could weather any storm that might come their way.

But godliness with contentment is great gain.
—1 Timothy 6:6

Lori learned quickly that she was bound to a man with severe anger-management problems who did not understand or value the sanctity of marriage. Her dream marriage was shattered in no time at all. Lori knew that God hated divorce, and as a committed Christian, she chose to stay in the abusive lifestyle for eleven years.

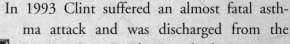

In 1993 Clint suffered an almost fatal asthma attack and was discharged from the Marine Corps with a medical retirement. The turmoil of realizing he wasn't fit for duty anymore took a great toll on Clint who became dangerously unpredictable. In spite of all Lori's efforts to cling to the Shepherd during the tumultuous marriage, her spirit was totally crushed. She felt she needed to take care of her three emotionally damaged children so she made preparations to leave Clint. Luke, thirteen and Chelsea, five, lived with Lori. In his anger, eleven-year-old Rashaan chose to live with his father.

Separation didn't have to mean divorce, and her desire to please God made Lori do everything possible over the next six years to save her marriage. Luke was relieved that his parents were not living together, but Rashaan remained angry and destructive. Chelsea began forming an ulcer due to her every effort to fix her parent's marriage.

Unfortunately, only Lori took the concept of reconciliation seriously. She learned that Clint had not only had at least one affair while they were separated but that he had also fathered a child. "I was furious," says Lori. "All this time I stayed faithful because I was still married. No matter how lonely I was, I knew seeking out a new relationship was wrong."

Lori struggled for years but finally signed the divorce papers. With three children ages nineteen, seventeen, and eleven, Lori despaired of ever finding another husband and prayed: *God, I'm now getting close to forty. You haven't got much time.* Confident that the Shepherd wouldn't leave her single for long, Lori set out to find her perfect partner.

Lori had not dated for twenty years. Back then she had frequented bars. She knew she wouldn't find a godly man there, so she continued to pray to the Shepherd. *Okay, God. I haven't dated for a very long time and, frankly, I have no idea where to start. I know You understand, and You feel sorry for me and You want to make this easy for me, right?*

If God be our God,
He will give us
peace in trouble.
—Thomas Watson

When no man appeared, Lori decided to take matters into her own hands. "I began an awkward journey into a world that was and still is very scary to me. I joined online Christian Web sites and discovered that not every man there is a Christian." It had been so long since any man flirted with Lori that she was simply giddy. But it didn't take Lori long to become disenchanted, and she stopped searching for a man online.

"Most of my free time was spent thinking about

ways to meet a man," admits Lori. "All I wanted was a man. I didn't want to grow old alone like my mother."

Each time she prayed to the Shepherd, the subject of a husband inevitably came up. *Don't I deserve a good marriage? Don't I deserve to have someone take care of me after all those years of abuse?* Questions so dominated her that she didn't focus on the relationships she already had in her life.

"In a few short years, Chelsea will be on her own," Lori says now. "I spent so much time fantasizing about Mr. Right that I did a lot of things wrong. In many ways I neglected my kids, especially Chelsea. Right now I want to be the best mother I can be to all my children."

Lori also wants to grow into a deeper relationship with the Shepherd. And so her story scripted by the Shepherd continues.

"I refuse to fret over my marital status anymore. Yes, I feel lonely and anxious at times: however, I usually have peace about my future."

Peace doesn't mean that Lori doesn't tell the Shepherd about her frustrations and fears. It does mean that eventually Lori calms down and listens to the Shepherd when he says, "But do you trust Me?"

She trusts Him because she now understands that the Shepherd knows His plans for her. He will be faithful to the end, and that's what Lori trusts.

"He always has what is best for me," Lori says with her newfound peace. "If it is for marriage, then it will come perfectly as He has already planned . If it is not marriage, then He will change me, so that my desire will be for something different."

An old song says that if you can't be with the one you love, then you should love the one you're with. Lori is honest about wanting someone to love and cherish, but she no longer places such a great emphasis on a possible future relationship. These days, growing deeper in love with the Shepherd and enjoying her children matters more to Lori than anything.

It's been a long story filled with difficult chapters, but today Lori is experiencing peace from the Shepherd. She doesn't want to be alone, but because Lori has learned to love the one she's with, even if she remains single, she knows she'll never really be alone.

A heart at peace gives life to the body,
but envy rots the bones.
—Proverbs 14:30

He who waits on God never waits too long.
—Chuck Wagner

O FOR A THOUSAND TONGUES TO SING

Charles Wesley

Jesus! the name that charms our fears,

That bids our sorrows cease;

'Tis music in the sinner's ears,

'Tis life, and health, and peace.

CHAPTER FIVE

THE SHEPHERD OF *Hope*

"HE RESTORES MY SOUL"

A FOUNDATION OF TRUTH

Growing up, Carl and Addie went to the same school, attended the same church, and sang in the choir together. It was more a matter of when they would marry, rather than if. Each was loved by the other's family, and if there was ever a couple that would make it to the end, they were it.

"I want a divorce," were the words that signaled the beginning of the end for what Carl had thought was a near-perfect marriage. Wondering what could have happened, Carl counted all they had going for them—thirteen years of marriage, two gorgeous daughters, a nice house, family vacations every year, and Carl's upwardly mobile career.

The LORD is good to those whose hope is in him, to the one who seeks him; it is good to wait quietly for the salvation of the LORD.
—Lamentations 3:25, 26

They struggled with money like most young families, but Addie returning to work solved that concern. And that's where things went wrong. Besides finding extra money for the family budget, Addie found a new man.

What Carl had hoped would be an amicable co-parenting of their daughters didn't happen. At the time of the divorce hearing, their oldest daughter, Suzanne, who was having problems with her mother and the boyfriend, wanted to live with Carl out of spite. Despite his desire to have her with him, Carl wanted Suzanne and her sister, Gayle, to grow up together and be there for each other through what he knew would be difficult years. "I talked her out of splitting up even though it broke my heart," says Carl sadly. And so both girls went with their mother. Carl had a large, two-bedroom apartment, and the girls stayed with their father most weekends.

Addie did as much as possible to distance Carl from his children, starting with Christmas at Disney World before the divorce was even final. "Being apart from my children was much worse than no longer being married to my wife," explains Carl who endured a divorce he never wanted. "The hurt of missing your children growing up cannot be replaced."

An Irish proverb says that hope is the physician of every misery, and Carl found hope for this particular misery through the Shepherd, the Great Physician. Carl thought he had a strong faith before Addie left, but the divorce shook his foundation. He had been raised in church and still attended with some frequency, but at first, he leaned on his mother, Mildred, for moral support.

"My mom was my rock," says Carl. "She helped me have hope. Mom listened, she gave me ideas on how to stay connected with my girls, and she prayed." Mildred kept him going in the beginning, but eventually, Carl's faith grew stronger.

As he leaned more on the Shepherd, Carl found that he revisited the scenes of his resentment less and less. What had been done to him mattered far less than making sure his daughters knew that he loved them. He spent as much time as possible with Suzanne and Gayle, but that became challenging after Addie moved with her boyfriend across country from Maryland to California. Visitation was restricted to the summers, with Carl paying for the expensive round-trip airline tickets.

Hope is the parent of faith.
—Cyrus A. Bartol

Since he could see Suzanne and Gayle only for a few precious weeks each year, Carl realized he would have to keep the lines of communication open. He sent self-addressed envelopes and stationery with check-off notes so he could keep abreast of what was happening in the girls' lives. He sent pictures and videos, called them by phone, and purchased small gifts—perfume, makeup, and clothes—at least monthly. Sometimes the gifts were never acknowledged, and he'd wonder if Addie had intercepted them and not given them to the girls, but Carl never stopped sending them. More importantly, he never gave up hope that eventually he would be able to see his girls every day.

Addie and her boyfriend, a struggling alcoholic, eventually married, but the blending of their families did not go well. Because of the drinking, their stepfather's abuse of Addie, and their mother's partiality to the other children, when Suzanne turned eighteen she refused to live with her mother.

By that time, Carl had remarried a wonderful woman his girls adored, and Suzanne moved in with them. Two years later, Gayle, accused of being a troublemaker, moved in with Carl at Addie's urging.

Carl says that from his earliest years his parents had built a foundation of truth in his life. That foundation included the truth that no matter what, the Shepherd would never abandon him. The eight years separated from his children were painful, but the Shepherd was there the entire time, giving him hope for a better future.

As much as he was tempted, Carl's desire that the three of them would be together never caused him to give Suzanne and Gayle false hope. When they realized the shallowness of their mother's love, Carl couldn't promise them they'd be able to move in with him. "All I could do was be the father I was called to be. I could never tell them something and then break their hearts by not fulfilling it. But I could have hope."

Carl never stopped hoping that the Shepherd would one day right what was terribly wrong. Today he has a loving relationship with both daughters and his three grandchildren. Like others who have had their faith strengthened through being single parents, Carl learned that when we have hope we can trust the Shepherd to work out situations, according to His will, no matter how unfair we think they are or how long it might take.

Let us hold unswervingly to the hope we profess, for he who promised is faithful.
—Hebrews 10:23

We go forward—because we hope.
—Arthur Jones

STANDING ON THE PROMISES

KELSO CARTER

Standing on the promises that cannot fail,

When the howling storms of doubt and fear assail,

By the living Word of God I shall prevail,

Standing on the promises of God.

Standing, standing,

Standing on the promises of God my Savior;

Standing, standing,

I'm standing on the promises of God.

CHAPTER SIX

THE SHEPHERD WHO *Directs*

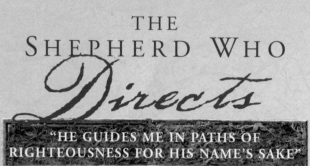

"HE GUIDES ME IN PATHS OF RIGHTEOUSNESS FOR HIS NAME'S SAKE"

TIED BY LOVE

"I need to dress for a job interview tomorrow," said Nicholas, my fifteen-year-old son, coming in from school one afternoon.

"You're getting a job?"

"No, we have to role-play in that life management skills class. I need a suit and tie."

Moving from Hawaii the previous year had meant leaving my sons' father, something I wondered if they would ever get over. Technically, I wasn't a single parent, but with their father five thousand miles away and their stepfather bedridden, I might as well have been.

For this God is our God for ever and ever; he will be our guide even to the end.
—Psalm 48:14

At over six feet tall, Nicholas lived in denim shorts, cotton shirts, and sports shoes. I didn't look in his closet, but knew we'd have to go shopping that afternoon, and, as usual, I had no extra money.

His announcement triggered a call to my friend, Carol. Her charity, Mustard Seed Furniture Bank, warehoused furniture and donated it to needy families throughout central Florida. We had moved to the area the previous year because of the financial burden of taking care of my terminally ill husband and Carol gave us furniture and other household items. She also had a clothing bank and when I called she said she had plenty of dress pants and shirts.

"Let's go, guys. They close at 5:00, and we're going to hit traffic."

With grumbles about why they had to wear other people's clothes the boys piled into the car and we set off to see what we could find.

"Mom, this stuff smells."

"Nicholas, please don't complain," I begged as we walked through the warehouse. "We can wash and iron everything, and it will be fine for tomorrow."

Carol had graciously said that I could take whatever fit the boys, so we dug through the piles like miners seeking the mother lode. The building had no air-conditioning, and the longer we stayed, the more our sweat poured. No matter what I suggested my sons pointed out problems: the wrong color, the wrong size, something old men would wear.

"It's just for an assignment," I snapped in frustration, grabbing a few shirts, slacks, and ties. "You never have to wear them again if you don't want to."

The ride home was a sullen affair. If I had to hear one more time how much they hated Florida, missed their friends, or wanted to be with Dad, I was going to scream. Couldn't they see I was doing all I could to make things work?

After dinner I handed Nicholas the interview clothes I had washed and ironed. Nothing was a perfect fit, and the collar on the dress shirt that almost worked was yellowed despite the bleach. It would have to do. I even promised he could wear the clothes to school but bring his regular attire in his backpack and switch after his first period.

"Go change, and show me how handsome you look."

With a roll of his eyes Nicholas stomped up the stairs.

I asked his brother to check on him when Nicholas had not appeared after a few minutes.

"He says he'll take a zero, Mom," said Justin delighting in his brother's discomfort. "He looks stupid, and he can't get the tie right. He's not coming down."

Why wasn't anything easy? All he had to do was to wear the stupid clothes. Was that too hard?

"Nicholas, please come down. Let's see how you look."

The pants were too short, the shirt baggy. As he made his way down the stairs, I prayed to the Shepherd. *Please Lord, help me through this. Help me to keep my temper no matter what he says.*

"This isn't going to work because you don't know how to tie a tie," he yelled, throwing the offending article on my desk next to where I was sitting.

"Honey, we'll figure it out."

"No, we won't!" screamed my son, towering over me, anger etched on his face. "We can't figure it out because Dad's not here. You're not a dad; you're just a mom. If you hadn't married David, we'd still be back home, and Dad could teach me how to do it."

We are here to help one another along life's journey.
—William Bennett

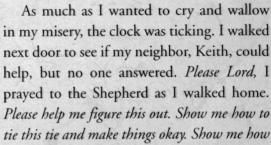

I realized this wasn't about secondhand clothes or not having money. His anger was about being separated from his father. He was right. I was just a mom, a terrible mom, and everything was my fault. Barely holding back my tears, I told the boys to go back upstairs.

As much as I wanted to cry and wallow in my misery, the clock was ticking. I walked next door to see if my neighbor, Keith, could help, but no one answered. *Please Lord,* I prayed to the Shepherd as I walked home. *Please help me figure this out. Show me how to tie this tie and make things okay. Show me how to be the mother my boys need.*

I went to retrieve the tie and looked at the computer. The Internet! There had to be a Web site where I could find directions. I logged on, went to Yahoo!, and typed in key words I prayed would get me to the perfect site.

In the scheme of things, directing a mother to a

site where she could learn about neckties might not be high on the Shepherd's list, but I also knew this wasn't about a necktie. This was about our family, and Nicholas had every right to feel like the two adults in his life had messed things up. My sons might not have a father living with them that could do all the guy things that I couldn't do, but I had a Father and he would get us through this.

I went to the first site, scrolled down, found a diagram, and clicked on what turned out to be directions on how to tie a necktie. I printed it out and taped it to the mirror of the downstairs bathroom.

"Nicholas, I figured it out," I called. "Could you come downstairs?"

I held my breath and asked the Shepherd for direction as I heard my firstborn pound as hard as possible on each step.

"I know you miss your dad, Nicholas. And I

wish things had worked out the way they should have and that we were still back home. But this is what we have to deal with, and we're going to make it, I promise."

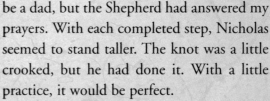

I stood behind my good-looking son and watched as he followed the instructions. I might not be a dad, but the Shepherd had answered my prayers. With each completed step, Nicholas seemed to stand taller. The knot was a little crooked, but he had done it. With a little practice, it would be perfect.

Looking at the handsome boy in the mirror, I saw a picture of the man he would soon be. I wrapped my arms around him and tried my best not to cry. I failed. He looked at me from the mirror and tried not to smile. He failed miserably.

Over the next few years, I needed the Shepherd's directions a lot as I raised my sons. But like the day Nicholas learned to knot his necktie, the Shepherd never let me down, and His directions helped us through many challenges. Today we are still tied by love.

Call to me and I will answer you and tell you great and unsearchable things you do not know.
—Jeremiah 33:3

The strength of a man consists in finding out the way God is going, and going that way.
—Henry Ward Beecher

ALL THE WAY MY SAVIOR LEADS ME

FANNY CROSBY

All the way my Savior leads me,

Cheers each winding path I tread,

Gives me grace for every trial,

Feeds me with the living bread.

Though my weary steps may falter

And my soul a-thirst may be,

Gushing from the Rock before me,

Lo! a spring of joy I see;

Gushing from the Rock before me,

Lo! a spring of joy I see.

CHAPTER SEVEN

THE SHEPHERD OF *Patience*

"EVEN THOUGH I WALK THROUGH THE VALLEY OF THE SHADOW OF DEATH"

TWO KITES

When my sons were younger, they loved to fly kites on the beach. One gorgeous day, I watched my two children, so alike yet so different, as they enjoyed themselves. Justin's kite danced upwards, the turquoise color blending with the ocean fronting the sandy beach. If we squinted, we could see the black-and-white appliqué shape of the killer whale on it as it rocketed to and fro. Justin's face was wreathed in a smile even brighter than the sun.

In sharp contrast was his brother, Nicholas, a dejected slump to his shoulders. His kite was lying

Let us not become weary in doing good, for at the proper time we will reap a harvest if we do not give up.
—Galatians 6:9

on the grassy field, looking even more forlorn than its owner. He was an ambitious boy, determined to fly the more complicated "trick" kite. Unlike the simple one Justin had, this kite had two strings and required either extensive experience or a second pair of hands.

I watched my first-born tenaciously trying to get the kite airborne. Each time he tried, Nicholas inched farther down the road to success. With each success, the kite whirled and danced in a way that showed how much more exciting and intricate the dance would be when the kite finally took flight. Each time it looked as though Nicholas would give up, I saw him square his shoulders. Conviction on his face told me he would succeed if he had to stay up all night.

As the day wore on his kite, faded by the sun to a worn, soft color, became dirty from repeatedly dropping to the ground. Just as I was ready to call it quits for the day, I saw the bedraggled kite swirl and dance across the sky as if it had taken on a life of its own. The joy on Nicholas' face was delightful. His patience had paid off.

A few years after Nicholas learned to fly his trick kite, he said something probably every teenager has said. I can't remember what set him off, but I can remember the hurt I felt as my defiant child, hands clenched, said, "I hate you!"

"I know you do," I patiently said, using both common sense and humor to deflect his anger. "That's your job as a teenager. I am simply giving you the tools you need to do your job more effectively." What could he say? With a look of disgust, he stomped off convinced I was the worst mother in the world.

St. Augustine once observed that patience is the companion of wisdom, and when I was raising my teenagers, I prayed to the Shepherd for both attributes.

You can learn many things from children. How much patience you have, for instance.
—Franklin P. Jones

When I have money to burn, I will hire a biblical scholar to find a verse in the Bible that I am sure is missing. Beginning in Genesis 16 there is a list of repercussions resulting from Adam and Eve eating the apple. In the original text, nestled somewhere between the pain of childbearing and working the land, must be the verse, "And you will raise teenagers."

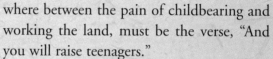

A Chinese proverb says that patience is power. With time and patience, the mulberry leaf becomes silk. I never set out to be a single parent, but, with the Shepherd's help, my children grew into silk—strong, flexible, and of great value. When I see a scrap of fabric dancing in the sky, taking unimaginable dives that defy explanation, I thank the Shepherd for giving me the patience to be the mother Nicholas and Justin needed.

A man's wisdom gives him patience;
it is to his glory to overlook an offense.
—Proverbs 19:11

Patience in the present, faith in the future,
and joy in the doing.
—George Perera

WHAT GOD HATH PROMISED

ANNIE J. FLINT

But God hath promised strength for the day,

Rest for the labor, light for the way,

Grace for the trials, help from above,

Unfailing sympathy, undying love.

CHAPTER EIGHT

THE SHEPHERD OF *Courage*

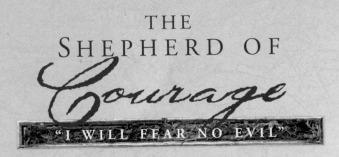

"I WILL FEAR NO EVIL"

NEW TRADITIONS

My husband moved out in September, and between paying legal fees and household expenses, I didn't have much money left for Christmas. Earlier that year, we had bought bunk beds for Nicholas and Justin but didn't have enough money for mattresses, so we placed a piece of plywood on each frame onto which we laid their futons. The futons were smaller than the twinsized frames leaving rims of wood exposed.

We are hard pressed on every side, but not crushed; perplexed, but not in despair, persecuted, but not abandoned, struck down but not destroyed.
—2 Corinthians 4:8, 9

After combing the newspaper for sales, practicality won out, and I bought mattresses on sale at the local furniture store. These would be their big gifts, but once I paid for the mattresses, I didn't have much left for presents. I did manage to buy socks, clothes, and some small things to place under the tree. I knew it wasn't a contest with their dad, but giving my children a nice Christmas that year was important.

Help me get through tomorrow, I prayed to the Shepherd when the children went to bed on Christmas Eve. "Help my kids not to be too disappointed." Needing an extra dose of courage, I had decided to fill the house with others celebrating the holiday alone. I explained to Nicholas and Justin that opening our home to others would make an enjoyable Christmas. They weren't enthusiastic about my plan, but I figured they would have other children to play with, and we'd all have a nice potluck meal.

The next morning my sons made the early-morning trek to the tree, anxious to see what Santa had brought. They made all the right noises when they opened their gifts, but their faces told a different story. They were less than enthusiastic over their mattresses.

"I have to frost cookies for this afternoon. Want to help?"

Spreading icing and sprinkles on sugar cookies was something that all four of us had enjoyed before divorce became a word in our vocabulary. This year, however, with Dad gone, the boys opted for television.

Trying to hold back tears of disappointment, I began my kitchen duties. A few minutes later, a motorcycle roared into the driveway. *That's funny. It's not even 9:00 and people aren't expected until 1:00.*

"Dad's here!" came the excited squeals from the living room. "It's Dad!"

What? This is my holiday with the kids. He gets them next week. I fought the rising anger since I could do nothing else.

"Hey, Nipper, Juice. Merry Christmas!" rang out the voice of the man who had promised to love and cherish me. The sound of his voice made me sick. How dare he come here today of all days? And then it got worse.

Courage is the power to let go of the familiar.
—Raymond Lindquist

Standing next to him was the girlfriend he'd said didn't exist. I knew he'd lied when he said he had no one else, but this was too much. Dressed in my ratty nightclothes with uncombed hair, I faced a perfectly coiffed and made-up woman bearing stacks of gifts.

Acting as if it were his right to be there, he introduced me to the woman as she gave each boy four or five beautifully wrapped packages. To her credit she seemed embarrassed, but that didn't make it any less humiliating. *Just get me through this. Give me the courage to not fall apart.*

"Can we open them, Dad?" Without waiting for an answer, the boys tore paper off the carefully chosen toys. Even then I could tell that she hadn't spent a lot of money, but it was more than I had been able to afford. Christmas was ruined. Unable to watch my children's excitement, I went back to the kitchen to get things ready for the open house I no longer wanted.

While the boys opened the gifts, Dad took his girlfriend on a tour of the house, showing off the woodwork he had stained and the new cabinets. I couldn't remember a more humiliating moment.

Eventually, they left, she on the back of his motorcycle, and I went to the bedroom to cry. Nicholas and Justin, engrossed in their holiday booty, were oblivious to their heart-broken mom. I cried until I had no more tears, and it was time to put the ham in the oven.

People began arriving after we showered and dressed. We were going to have a good time, even if it killed me. My whole reason for having an open house that day was to give me the courage to face our first Christmas alone, but the Shepherd had other plans.

People came laden, not only with casseroles and desserts but with presents. Everyone had thought to bring something for either the boys or me. What began as a meager Christmas turned into a joyful one, but the gifts were the least of our blessings. It had been a long time since laughter rang in our house, and it was fun seeing my kids enjoy other children and play with their toys.

Talking to other single parents that day, I got the courage I needed to get through the divorce. I realized that fancy gifts weren't as important to Nicholas and Justin as being raised by a mother who had the courage to trust the Shepherd in every area of her life. I knew that somehow the Shepherd would give me the courage to get through each day. The three of us would begin new traditions of our own.

"Time for bed," I told the kids that night after everyone left. They were so tired they didn't even argue. After donning their pajamas, the boys climbed into their bunks. I stood in the doorway and listened to the chatter between the two brothers. As I took the first step into the room, I heard words that still warm my heart.

"I love my bed," said Justin, kissing the Star Wars sheets and spreading out his arms to hug the mattress.

"Me, too, Justin," came his brother's sleepy response.

Wait for the L*ORD; be strong and*
take heart and wait for the L*ORD.*
—Psalm 27:14

Optimism is the foundation of courage.
—Nicholas Murray Butler

HOW FIRM A FOUNDATION

ATTRIBUTED VARIOUSLY TO JOHN KEENE, JOHN KIRKHAM, AND JOHN KEITH

Fear not, I am with thee; O be not dismayed,

For I am thy God, and will still give thee aid;

I'll strengthen thee, help thee, and cause thee to stand.

Upheld by My righteous, omnipotent hand.

CHAPTER NINE

THE SHEPHERD OF *Friends*

"FOR YOU ARE WITH ME"

THE CEREAL AND MILK MIRACLE

As a single mom, I panicked every month when bill-paying time reared its ugly head. How could I spread so little money so far? It was routine for my children to preface each request for whatever they wanted or needed to buy with, "Mom, I know you don't have the money but . . . ," and I grew increasingly frustrated at having to say no.

A friend loves at all times and a brother is born for adversity.
—Proverbs 17:17

One harried day, everything that could go wrong did from the moment I awoke. Walking in from a fruitless check of the mailbox that afternoon, I said, "Right. The check's in the mail." As the owner of a small marketing firm, I was at the mercy of clients paying their bills on time. They rarely did, and with only a handful of change left till I got my child-support check, I didn't know what to do. I heard the phone ringing, so I dashed into the house. It was Melanie, my friend from Los Angeles.

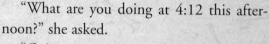

"What are you doing at 4:12 this afternoon?" she asked.

"Going crazy, trying to figure out what to fix for dinner."

"Why not meet the 4:12 American Airlines flight from L.A.? There's a box on it for you. Gotta run; call you later."

"Great!" I grumbled to myself. "That's the middle of rush hour." I continued my tirade, all the time trying to figure out what could possibly be in that box. Whatever it contained, it was not going to solve my immediate problems.

After school, I loaded my eight- and nine-year-old sons into the car for an airport run over the mountains. Somehow the snail-paced traffic moved, and we made it to our destination where I squeezed into a no-loading space and dashed into the baggage section. My frustration mounted as the conveyor belt went round and round with luggage of every size, shape, and description, and not one box in sight. One minute became five, then five became ten until finally, at long last, seventeen long minutes of unfruitful scrutiny paid off. I spotted the box.

As I fought through the crowd to claim the parcel, I saw three more identical boxes following the first one, all labeled in Melanie's precise handwriting. Instead of being thankful for the additional boxes, I was enraged. How did she think I could fit four huge boxes into my car? I didn't even have three dollars to rent a luggage cart, so I continued mumbling and complaining with each trip to the car. After repositioning the boxes umpteen times, I was ready to explode.

For the entire trip home, I listened to the children's pleas to open the boxes, interspersed with their demands to stop at McDonald's. We were all tired and hungry, and I didn't have a clue what to have for dinner. I wish I could tell you that I prayed for the Shepherd to reveal His plan, but I was too busy yelling at drivers and grumbling about all that I didn't have.

If a friend is in trouble, don't annoy him by asking if there is anything you can do. Think up something appropriate and do it.
—Edgar Watson Howe

The boys tumbled out of the car, each struggling with a box. Then, using the sharpest implement I could find in a drawer full of dull kitchen utensils, I opened the first one. I stared as the children whooped with joy. Cereal. Cartons and cartons of cereal.

After lugging the remaining boxes into the house, I gazed in growing consternation at what seemed to be the contents of a small convenience store on my livingroom floor. I listened to the squeals of delight emanating from the children and wondered what on earth had prompted Melanie to send all this stuff. Half of it was sugar laden. Why not take an IV needle and just shoot sucrose into their veins? How was I going to store all this in Hawaii's humid climate? Where was I going to get the money to buy milk for the cereal?

Continuing to mutter under my breath, I tried to stop the boys from opening all the cereal as they looked for hidden prizes. With cereal so expensive, it was probably worth a mint, but it did not solve my dinner predicament.

I was trying to control the situation when the phone rang. Melanie was calling to explain that triple-coupon days had allowed her to buy all of this for less than ten dollars. I thanked her as enthusiastically as I could while silently begging the Shepherd to explain Himself. Just how did this solve my dinner problems?

Just then I heard a car brake, looked out the window, and saw my friend, Barbara.

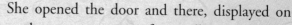

"I can't stay," she said. "I'm in a hurry. I just went to the food bank and am on my way home. My boys are allergic to this, and I thought maybe you could use it."

She opened the door and there, displayed on the car seat, were four gallon containers. As I gaped at the milk, I began to laugh. Barbara didn't get milk every time she went to the food bank, yet on that day, the exact day I would have a use for four gallons, the Shepherd gave her exactly what I needed.

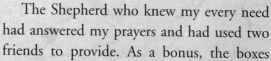

The Shepherd who knew my every need had answered my prayers and had used two friends to provide. As a bonus, the boxes from Melanie were filled with other packaged foods previously on the too expensive list that I could use for several meals and snacks. Even if I didn't receive a client check, we had enough food to last until the first of the month when the child-support money arrived.

Despite not praying and how miserable I'd made everyone as I ruminated on my own disappointments and trials, the Shepherd showed how much He cared for my family by directing both Barbara and Melanie to be a part of His plan for our lives.

I've never forgotten how the Shepherd used two friends and something as simple as cereal and milk to get me through a difficult time. He never came through with half a plan; it was always complete, and sometimes he used friends to help.

We live by faith, not by sight.
—2 Corinthians 5:7

A gift in season is a double favor to the needy.
—Publilius Syrus

WE WALK BY FAITH

FANNY CROSBY

We walk by faith, but not alone,

Our Shepherd's tender voice we hear

And feel His hand within our own,

And know that He is always near.

CHAPTER TEN

THE SHEPHERD WHO *Comforts*

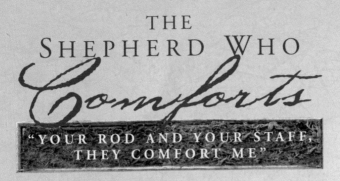

"YOUR ROD AND YOUR STAFF, THEY COMFORT ME"

TWO THANKSGIVINGS

I recently got an e-mail from a friend relating a story about a special Thanksgiving. Mary's husband was away doing graduate study for a year, and every cent she earned as a teacher was stretched to the limit. Kathy, her fourteen-year-old, had come home from school two days before Thanksgiving with the news that one of her friends wasn't going to celebrate the holiday because her mother couldn't afford it.

For just as the sufferings of Christ flow over into our lives, so also through Christ our comfort overflows.
—2 Corinthians 1:5

"What are we going to do to help, Mom?"

Mary had taught her kids to help others. But to help someone else now when she barely had enough to provide for her own family didn't make sense. How could Mary explain to Kathy that she was serving the turkey she had purchased on sale for their Thanksgiving dinner? They couldn't afford to help another family.

In a few seconds, Mary knew the answer. The Shepherd would have to provide another turkey for their Thanksgiving dinner.

"Well, let's gather up some things and then run to the store to pick up a few extras." Mary sent her son, Matt, to the freezer in the garage to get the turkey and vegetables. She had a bag of potatoes and cranberry sauce in the pantry. Kathy chose pies and stuffing from the grocery store. The single mother's eyes glistened with tears when Mary and her children delivered her Thanksgiving feast.

A few days later, Mary lifted the heavy lid of their old freezer chest and peered inside at bags of frozen wild blackberries and vegetables from their garden. As she started to reach in to get a bag of broccoli, Mary's hand stopped in midair. Nestled among the packages of green beans and corn was a frozen turkey.

Rivulets of tears trickled down Mary's face when she realized what had probably happened. Knowing that because of their generosity Mary's family wouldn't have a turkey for Thanksgiving, a friend must have secretly replaced their gift with a second turkey. Although she never found out the donor's identity, she and her children never forgot the joy of providing comfort to a single mother in need. Whoever put that turkey into their freezer got that same joy.

"A single sunbeam is enough to drive away many shadows."
—Francis of Assisi

Reading Mary's e-mail brought back a Thanksgiving memory of my own. After my divorce, I was a single mom with two sons. Eventually, I remarried, only to have my new husband become ill soon after. Now I was back with the challenges of a single parent plus caring for a terminally ill husband.

When I needed it most, the Shepherd sent me a comforting note. It was going to be a lean Thanksgiving that year, and I prayed to the Shepherd not only for enough food for a dinner, but also for His comfort. I was weary of the endless struggles.

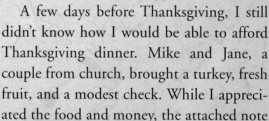

A few days before Thanksgiving, I still didn't know how I would be able to afford Thanksgiving dinner. Mike and Jane, a couple from church, brought a turkey, fresh fruit, and a modest check. While I appreciated the food and money, the attached note gave me the most comfort. "Dearest Carmen, We hope you will always feel comfortable enough with us to let us know what we can do to help you. We love you, Carmen, for your heart and your courage! The Lord is well served by your struggles and testimony for Him. Take care, dearest Carmen, and always remember how much we treasure you as a friend and a soldier for Christ."

Once again the Shepherd of comfort had answered my prayers. In her note, Jane assured me of her friendship, acknowledged my pain, and showed me how God was using my struggles in her life. She also gave me permission to let her know when I had needs. She didn't preach or try to diminish what was happening in my life. She just loved me.

Maya Angelou says, "When we give cheerfully and accept gratefully, everyone is blessed." Both Mary and I were blessed and comforted by people being prompted by the Shepherd.

The LORD is good, a refuge in times of trouble.
He cares for those who trust in him.
—Nahum 1:7

Regardless of the need, God comforts.
—Charles R. Swindoll

MAKE ME A BLESSING

IRA WILSON

Give as 'twas given to you in your need,

Love as the Master loved you;

Be to the helpless a helper indeed,

Unto your mission be true.

Make me a blessing, make me a blessing—

Out of my life may Jesus shine;

Make me a blessing, O Savior, I pray,

Make me a blessing to someone today.

CHAPTER ELEVEN

THE SHEPHERD OF *Protection*

"YOU PREPARE A TABLE BEFORE ME IN THE PRESENCE OF MY ENEMIES"

SOMETHING SIMPLE

This was just like the dream she'd had the previous week, Nanette thought. That night she had awakened with a start, gasping for air, drenched in sweat. This time it wasn't a dream though, and Nanette sat like a piece of petrified wood as her husband, Ben, thrust a gun in her face.

But whoever listens to me will live in safety and be at ease, without fear of harm.
—Proverbs 1:33

Lord, I want to live. I want to see my children grow up. Please protect me. Nanette prayed silently, knowing only the Shepherd could help her.

Nanette had asked for a separation because of Ben's drinking and lifestyle more suited to a barfly than a married father of two young sons. She could no longer subject her children or herself, for that matter, to the battleground their home had become.

After telling Ben she was leaving, Nanette waited to see how he would react. She breathed a small sigh of relief as he began tossing clothes into a suitcase. Then, without warning, Ben, a demented look in his eyes, stopped short.

"I'm not leaving, and if you leave me, I'll just have to kill you." With calculated calmness, Ben closed and locked both bedroom doors and each window, then walked into the large closet. Almost as in a trance, Ben reached for the top shelf and pulled down his .38 caliber Magnum and a box of shells. Turning toward Nanette, he began to load the gun.

Nanette measured her life with each click as she heard the bullets fall into place as he loaded the chambers. *The dream was a warning!* Closing her eyes and praying for the Shepherd's protection, Nanette remembered that in the dream her screaming had been what had caused Ben to aim the gun at her stomach and pull the trigger. *Stay silent.*

The silence surrounded Nanette like the calm before a storm. As she waited to see what Ben would do she heard the Shepherd's voice: *Tell him you love him.*

Though she still loved the father of her children, she knew her marriage was over. Fear mingled with sadness as she spoke the words that no doubt saved her life, "I love you, Ben."

Ben held the gun in midair, as he stared at Nanette. Trembling, he lowered the gun. Shaken, Ben sat next to Nanette and told her about his plan of killing her if she ever tried to leave him.

Nanette was used to Ben's violent behavior, but this time he had crossed a line that signaled the end. It was bad enough when he had pounded the walls in a rage. He had even threatened to drop-kick their dog like a football on one occasion. But the violence had escalated to the point where Nanette knew she had to get out or lose her life.

O God, never suffer us to think that we can stand by ourselves, and not need Thee.
—John Donne

Ben was her constant shadow that endless weekend. Monday morning Nanette left for work with her two boys, four and seven. As she sat in the day care parking lot watching her two precious sons walk inside, a wave of grief overwhelmed her. The precarious dam she had erected that weekend broke, and a flood of tears fell. Words she had memorized years before in vacation bible school broke through: "Even though I walk through the valley of the shadow of death, I will fear no evil, for you are with me." That snippet of Psalm 23 gave Nanette the assurance that the Shepherd would protect her and the boys.

Eventually, Nanette did move with David and Donnie to a safe place, but they had left in such a hurry that she'd taken nothing with her except a few belongings she had hurriedly loaded into her compact station wagon. *Gone. Everything is gone—my husband, my clothes, my life . . . even my dog.*

Nanette managed to get a full-sized mattress that she and the boys slept on in the townhouse she had moved to, hoping that Ben wouldn't find them. Upended cardboard boxes that held the dishes she had managed to salvage became tables where they ate their meals while sitting on the floor.

Nanette, almost numb from grief and fear, cried out of loneliness and self-pity. *What would happen if Ben found them? Who would protect them? No one cared if they lived or died.*

Had Nanette only asked, she would have found the Shepherd had people who would support her. But she couldn't bring herself to go the short distance to a nearby church for help. Her part-time secretarial job barely paid their expenses. Child support wasn't an option because that might create a trail for Ben to follow to the new town she had chosen when she fled from him. Fearful for their safety, she opted for food stamps.

Christmas drew near, and, despite her growing depression, Nanette tried to create a celebration for David and Donnie. Between the tree dying before Christmas day and the meager display underneath, it was anything but festive.

Since the months when Nanette fled for her life, the Shepherd's promise that He would protect her family had kept her going. But she couldn't help wondering if protection didn't mean more than just sparing their lives. Where was the Shepherd's protection for everything else?

In the new year, a coworker, realizing how depressed Nanette had become, gave her a kitten. When she got home that evening, Nanette placed the small orange-colored ball of fur in Donnie's lap. His eyes widened and a smile curved upwards as he put his head on the kitten's stomach.

"What are you doing, honey?" Nanette asked, watching Donnie's strange reaction.

His eyebrows furrowed in deep thought, and then he said, "My kitty has swallowed a motorcycle! I hear it in his tummy."

Robert Fulghum said, "We are the only creatures that both laugh and weep. I think it's because we are the only creatures that see the difference between the way things are and the way they might be." On that day, Nanette, who had wept for the way things might have been, laughed out loud. Seeing Donnie's childlike delight in something simple gave Nanette a vision for what might one day be.

The Shepherd had answered her prayers, and Nanette knew that no matter what challenges might come, He would always protect her little family.

I will lie down and sleep in peace, for you alone,
O Lord, make me dwell in safety.
—Psalm 4:8

Wherever you are, whatever your circumstances may be, whatever misfortune you may have suffered, the music of your life has not gone. It's inside you—if you listen to it, you can play it.
—Nido Qubein

STAND BY ME

CHARLES A. TINDLEY

In the midst of tribulation,
Stand by me (stand by me);
In the midst of tribulation,
Stand by me (stand by me);
When the hosts of hell assail,
And my strength begins to fail,
Thou Who never lost a battle,
Stand by me (stand by me).

CHAPTER TWELVE

THE SHEPHERD WHO *Heals*

"YOU ANOINT MY HEAD WITH OIL"

WHY ME?

I saw the tableau and knew that the stage had been deliberately set. A judge had ordered my husband to move out of the house in one week. Now came the devastating task of telling our six- and eight-year-old sons, Nicholas and Justin. I knew I had walked into an ambush when I saw the three of them already seated. Nick sat on the sofa, his arm around each of my sons. The only place left to sit was the rocking chair across from them.

> *Forgive us our debts, as we also have forgiven our debtors.*
> —Matthew 6:12

"A lady judge in a black robe told Daddy he can't live here anymore," said one of my sons.

I couldn't believe what I was hearing. This was so unfair. Of course that was not why I had gotten a restraining order and was now facing a custody battle destined to break both my heart and my bank account.

"The lawyer told the judge that your mom's pastor said I was a bad man so I have to leave."

Speechless, I watched my children's questioning looks before they dissolved into puddles of tears. Nick's viciousness complicated an already horrific job of telling the boys about the divorce. Now he cuddled Nicholas and Justin and told them he would always be there and how much he loved them. He painted me as the outsider, the one who had destroyed our family. I vowed never to forgive him.

Somehow we survived the next week and the subsequent stormy months but not without our children being scarred by the deplorable reality and the way they learned the news.

Nightly phone calls and every other weekend

and midweek visits became power-play opportunities in an unfair game of he said/she said. Each week the boys came home with some comment skewed by their dad in the telling. I certainly wasn't blameless. At times I painted their father in a less-than-favorable light, but still, what he was doing was unforgivable.

Since every phone call was a battlefield, the only way we could communicate with any calm was through our attorneys. Eventually, things changed. Not overnight and not without many more years of warfare, but they did change.

One day, sitting on one of the most beautiful beaches in the world, I cried until I was dry. I screamed silently to the Shepherd, *Why me?*

That night before going to bed, I poured out my disappointments and unhappiness in a poem. I am an optimistic person by nature, so it didn't take me long to move onto the joys in my life.

Penning the good things led me to write about the Shepherd and how thankful I was for Him.

The next morning I woke up to an angry phone call about child support or visitation, I don't remember exactly. What I do remember is the Shepherd's voice: *Pray for him.*

The glory of Christianity is to conquer by forgiveness.
—William Blake

Pray for *him*? He didn't deserve my prayers. Hadn't he forbidden me to use his last name after the divorce? The first Mother's Day after I'd taken back my maiden name, Justin presented me with a certificate to "Carmen Lil, World's Best Mother." My son didn't even know how to spell his mother's name. I was supposed to forgive that? And what about the way he'd broken the news to the kids? I had adored his family, and he had forced me to break off any communication with them. He didn't deserve my prayers or my forgiveness.

Throughout the day, I kept thinking about the Shepherd's call to pray for my ex-husband. In the beginning, I prayed for his health. I figured that if he got sick, he couldn't earn money to pay child support. I could pray for that.

A week after I started praying for Nick, self-serving prayers if the truth be told, we had a missions' fair. *Nick is your mission field.* This time I understood what the Shepherd was saying. I wasn't supposed to pray only for his health or that he became a better person. I needed to pray for his salvation.

It really is impossible to remain angry at people when you pray for them. Whenever we exchanged angry words I prayed for him as soon as I hung up. I prayed for him to be a good father, but I also prayed for him to believe in the Shepherd.

It took many years, but the Shepherd has healed my anger and taken away the bitterness that lived in my heart. Nick and I sat together at Justin's high-school graduation. At first I thought he was putting on an act, but since that day, not one shred of animosity hangs between us. Two years later, we celebrated when Nicholas received his college diploma, and recently, we clapped together as he graduated from his navy basic training. I have no doubt that one day we will stand together in the maternity ward and take turns holding our grandchildren.

Thanks to the Shepherd, I realized that my job wasn't to change Nick or to fix what was broken. No, my job was to pray for Nick and let the Shepherd take care of the rest. I also had to confess my sins and accept the Shepherd's forgiveness. And from forgiveness came healing.

Why Me?

I gaze at the serene blue waters and wonder, Why me?
I ponder my shattered hopes and dreams and wonder, Why me?
I recall happier times, and wonder, Why me?

Sitting on the barren beach with waves splashing against the shore,
I feel as empty as the horizon.
As a lone tear drips off my chin and splashes onto the rocks,
I believe I can fill the ocean with the tears I have shed.

When my turbulent emotions become placid,
I think of my beautiful sons and wonder, Why me?
I reflect on my health, my family and friends and wonder, Why me?
I am blessed by thoughts of my church and wonder, Why me?

My mind fairly races with the joys of my life
I have somehow forgotten in my self-pity.

I consider a God so great that He sent His son to die on the cross for me,
and I wonder, Why me?
I am grateful that as Jesus hung on the cross
He didn't say, Why me?

A time to kill and a time to heal, a time to tear down and a time to build.
—Ecclesiastes 3:3

Forgiveness is not an occasional act; it is a permanent attitude.
—Martin Luther King, Jr.

MY FAITH HAS FOUND A RESTING PLACE

Eliza E. Hewitt
(Lidie H. Edmunds, Eliza's pseudonym)

My faith has found a resting place,

Not in a manmade creed;

I trust the ever living One,

That He for me will plead.

My great Physician heals the sick,

The lost He came to save;

For me His precious blood He shed,

For me His life He gave.

CHAPTER THIRTEEN

THE SHEPHERD OF *Blessings*

"MY CUP OVERFLOWS"

MEGAN'S CAR

An unplanned pregnancy pushed forward a marriage that might never have occurred. Megan was determined to make the marriage work, and she and Paul looked forward to the birth of their child. But their marriage never made its way from rocky to smooth. Paul's temper escalated and his behavior grew increasingly worrisome to the young wife and mother.

"The earth is the LORD's, and everything in it, the world, and all who live in it."
—Psalm 24:1

With more angry words than kind, with more erratic actions than calm, the marriage ended a few years later. Megan left college in California and returned home to Hawaii with her two children, Jaime and Zoe. Without a college degree and two children under three to care for, Megan hacked her way through the red tape of social-service programs. It was a humbling experience, but it wouldn't last forever.

Megan knew that to adequately provide for her children she would have to finish her education.

She enrolled in a program that would prepare her to work with the hearing impaired. Her days were filled with learning American Sign Language, a part-time job, and the daily activities of being mommy to two active children.

Megan also needed a strong support system for her little family, so she returned to the church of her youth. Sessions with the associate pastor, a gifted counselor, helped Megan grow beyond the hurts of a broken marriage and the wrongs she had endured. Another blessing were the loving friendships and wise counsel of older women. The Shepherd used one of those women to bless Megan in a special way.

Transportation is something we take for granted until the threat of being without it looms. Then it becomes one of the most critical things in our lives. A couple of years after Megan returned home, she found herself in that position. Her compact car was almost held together with duct tape and could not pass the safety check the next week.

"Jaime, we need to ask God to help us," explained Megan. "Mommy can't go to work, or school or everything else I need to do without a car. Let's pray, okay?"

With the quiet confidence of someone who has had her prayers answered in miraculous ways, Megan prayed but left the details up to the Shepherd. He could either allow the car to pass inspection, or He could give her a new car. It was His choice.

A few days later, Margi and Jim, a couple from church visited Megan. They were going through their own financial challenges, but Margi and Jim

*I am only one;
but still I am one.
I cannot do
everything, but
still I can do
something. I will
not refuse to do
the something
I can do.*
—Helen Keller

listened to the Shepherd as He urged them to help Megan. The three chatted for a while, and then Margi handed Megan a pretty little gift bag.

"Why are you giving me a present?"

"Just open it." Margi was excited to see Megan's reaction.

"Oh, my!" screamed Megan when she pulled out keys and the registration for a new car.

"You can't afford this," Megan protested. She had asked the Shepherd to bless her with transportation, but she knew that Margi and Jim had their own money woes.

After Megan had recovered, Margi and Jim said they had communicated to others in the church how she could not go to school or care for her two children without a car.

"God has lots of cars, Megan," said Margi as she explained the plan that had resulted in Megan's car. "He also has lots of money. All we had to do was to get some of God's money to buy one of God's cars."

"But where did you get the money?"

When Margi heard that Megan's car was about to get taken off the road, she knew she had to help. Jim found a reliable used car for three thousand dollars, which they couldn't afford to buy, but they could spare one hundred dollars from their overburdened budget. In a short space of time, Margi and Jim found twenty-nine other church members to give one hundred dollars toward the purchase of the car.

Megan couldn't wait to tell Jaime how the Shepherd had blessed them with a car. Better than the car, of course, was the blessing of thirty friends who banded together to help this single mother. The Shepherd's blessing also allowed those thirty people to experience the joy of giving. Those who helped learned that it really was more blessed to give than to receive.

Each man should give what he has decided in his heart to give, not reluctantly or under compulsion, for God loves a cheerful giver.
—2 Corinthians 9:7

Our prayers should be for blessings in general, for God knows best what is good for us.
—Socrates

WE GATHER TOGETHER

EDUARD KREMSER

We gather together to ask the Lord's blessing;

He chastens and hastens His will to make known.

The wicked oppressing now cease from distressing.

Sing praises to His Name; He forgets not His own.

CHAPTER FOURTEEN

THE SHEPHERD WHO *Loves*

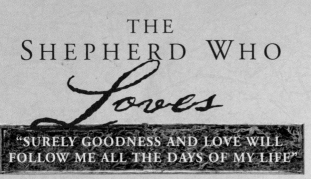

"SURELY GOODNESS AND LOVE WILL FOLLOW ME ALL THE DAYS OF MY LIFE"

SUNDAY SIT-DOWN

For years she had struggled to make their marriage work, but Cedric had taken the decision out of Diane's hands. He'd filed the papers, and Diane faced not only a divorce but also a possible custody battle. As if that weren't enough, the threat of outsourcing made Diane wonder how long she'd have her job now that a good income was critical. At times she wanted to stay in bed rather than face the day, but with three daughters still at home, she continued as best she could.

How wide and long and high and deep is the love of Christ.
—Ephesians 3:18

The year had been difficult in many ways, and while Diane didn't seem miserable, she certainly wasn't as cheerful as she used to be. My niece, fifteen-year-old Natalie, wanted to do something special to show how much she loved her mother, so she decided to create an event using her newly discovered culinary skills. "Mamma, can I have a party? I don't mean for kids or anything," Natalie hastened to add. "I want to do all the cooking and invite your friends."

With Diane's approval, Natalie planned what she later called her "Sunday Sit-Down." She invited four of her mother's friends and my other sisters, Debbie and Patricia.

The ladies gathered at Diane's house the first Sunday in December, not knowing what to expect. What they experienced was far more than they ever dreamed a fifteen-year-old could do for her mother.

"I like to cook," explains Natalie when asked about the festive day. "I like doing things efficiently, and I felt like having a party. Most of all,

I wanted to do something nice for my mom since she was going through a hard time."

"These chocolate truffles are great," said Debbie. "Where did you buy them?"

"I made them, Aunt Debbie," came Natalie's proud reply and shy smile. "I made everything."

"Everything!" exclaimed the women in disbelieving chorus. Chip and dip and vegetables on a platter were one thing, but the sausage and bacon wraps were delicious enough to have been made by a professional caterer.

Natalie's luscious desserts—chocolate raspberry torte, pecan puffs, and pecan delight—drew praise from the ladies. Everyone enjoyed an assortment of beverages that afternoon as they ate and laughed while Natalie beamed.

Proverbs 31:28 says that the children of a godly woman will call their mother blessed. That's exactly what happened when Natalie purchased, prepared, and served refreshments to seven godly

Love is the greatest refreshment in life.
—Pablo Picasso

women. Only a loving mother could have raised such a generous daughter who would give up her money, as well as her time, to tell her mother she is a blessing.

The great philosopher, Sophocles, said, "Children are the anchors that hold a mother to life." As much as Diane loves the four anchors in her life, she loves the Shepherd even more.

"I never doubted that God loves me and always will," says Diane. "But Natalie's gift, along with special blessings from all my children, remind me of that love."

I am sure that as Diane goes through the challenges of divorce and single parenting she will remember Natalie's Sunday Sit-Down and the Shepherd's love.

This is the message you heard from the beginning:
We should love one another.
—1 John 3:11

The supreme happiness in life is the
conviction that we are loved.
—Victor Hugo

HE HIDETH MY SOUL

FANNY CROSBY

He hideth my soul in the cleft of the rock

That shadows a dry, thirsty land;

He hideth my life in the depths of His love,

And covers me there with His hand,

And covers me there with His hand.

CHAPTER FIFTEEN

THE SHEPHERD OF Joy

"AND I WILL DWELL IN THE HOUSE OF THE LORD FOREVER"

SACRIFICE FLY

When I was a little girl, my dad made us watch him play softball for the post office or Knights of Columbus leagues. My siblings and I would sit in the harsh Kansas sun, bored, wanting to be anywhere but in that treeless park. I found baseball about as exciting as watching nail polish dry, but as long as my dad lived, I didn't dare bad-mouth baseball in his presence.

But he who stands firm to the end will be saved.
—Matthew 24:13

We'd play with other kids held hostage by their middle-aged fathers. Staying within the perimeters of some predetermined, invisible fence allowed us some level of freedom and access to under-the-bleachers hideouts, swings, and hot slides that burned our bare legs.

I don't remember my mom going to Daddy's games either before or after they separated when I was nine years old. I didn't hear much about his moving to a different house and the eight of us staying with my mom. Now that I think about it, things must have been desperate for a woman with eight children, five of them under the age of ten, to get a divorce in the 1960s. Years later I learned that my dad suffered from an undiagnosed chemical imbalance that affected his ability to be the husband and dad we needed him to be. He loved us, but my mom had to make difficult choices that affected all of us.

For years I thought of my mom as the heroine with creative parenting skills who sacrificed so her eight children had enough to eat and got a good education. She made sure we did our homework and stayed out of trouble and on the college-bound track. But she wasn't the only one who sacrificed. She wasn't the only hero.

Although my parents were divorced I saw my dad every day. Today there are visitation schedules, and children alternate their time between both parents. In our case, Mom worked a three-to-eleven shift, and my dad came over every evening after work when she was away. As an adult, I can imagine how awkward it must have been to be a visitor in what used to be your home, but my dad sacrificed his feelings to be with us.

Daddy was a handsome man who probably could have gone out every night of the week with some beautiful woman. Instead, he spent time with us more evenings than not, and if he did go bowling or play baseball, we often went along.

Daddy sacrificed many other things over the years. He gave Mom two hundred dollars every month for his child support and he never missed a payment. He kept up until the day he died, twenty years after the twins turned eighteen.

When he could have been out with friends, my dad sacrificed time to build kitchen cabinets or come to our concerts. He helped us with our homework and watched television with us. Of course, I don't think he considered any of these things as sacrifices. It's just what you do when you're a dad.

Self-sacrifice is the real miracle out of which all the reported miracles grow.
—Ralph Waldo Emerson

I remember a softball game once where it was the bottom of the ninth, scores tied, two outs, bases loaded. The home-run king was up at bat. A whispered conversation between the batter and the coach left our prize hitter shaking his head with a none-too-pleased scowl on his face. His posture spoke volumes as he argued with the coach.

A sacrifice fly enables a runner on third base to score after a pop fly is caught by an outfielder. For the batter, it's an easy out. But, at the bottom of the ninth with the bases loaded with only one run needed to win, the coach ordered the batter to hit a sacrifice fly.

That day, an outfielder, his glove shielding his eyes from the sun, backed farther into the field, glove extended, and caught the pop fly. The runner on third, knowing victory depended on his ability to make it home before being tagged out, slid into home.

I consider both of my single parents team players rather than home-run kings. They each had flaws, but they also possessed one shining attribute: they loved their children passionately. I also think of them as sacrifice flies because our needs came first.

I never set out to be a single parent. I came from a single-parent home where all eight children grew up to be loving, joyful men and women of God, and that is nothing short of miraculous.

Each of my parents gave me things that make me uniquely me. I inherited my dad's build and his singing voice. I got his curly hair and his temper. I no longer hate the former, but I am still struggling with the latter. I learned to juggle finances from my mother, but I'm a better cook. I also inherited her patience and ability to parent boys. Best of all, from both of them I learned to be honest, to laugh, and to enjoy life.

I've heard it said that it doesn't matter whether you win or lose but how you play the game. That might be true in baseball, but it is definitely not true in life. How you play the game determines if you win or lose for eternity, and both my parents taught me that to win I had to accept the ultimate sacrifice the Shepherd made when He died for my sins.

Daddy is already with the Shepherd, enjoying his mansion, and he probably has his own private baseball diamond in the backyard. My mother is enjoying the new house my sister built for her, and hopefully, it will be many years before she moves into whatever mansion the Shepherd has set aside for her. Because of their legacy and the sacrifices they made, all eight of us, and hopefully our children and grandchildren, will join them one day and together we will sing praises to the Shepherd of joy.

You need to persevere so that when you have done the will of God, you will receive what he has promised.
—Hebrews 10:36

Heaven, the treasury of everlasting joy.
—William Shakespeare

NEARER, MY GOD, TO THEE

SARAH FLOWER ADAMS

Or, if on joyful wing,

Cleaving the sky,

Sun, moon, and stars forgot,

Upward I fly;

Still all my song shall be,

Nearer, my God, to Thee,

Nearer, my God, to Thee,

Nearer to Thee!

Before you were conceived, I wanted you.
Before you were born, I loved you.
Before you were here an hour, I would die for you.
This is the miracle of life.
—Maureen Hawkins

With the Shepherd's help, **Carmen Leal** raised two wonderful sons as a single mother. She is the author and creator of *The Twenty-Third Psalm for Caregivers, The Twenty-Third Psalm for Those Who Grieve,* and *The Twenty-Third Psalm for the Brokenhearted.* A storyteller who has a dramatic testimony, she is a popular presenter at women's retreats, church groups, conventions, and conferences.

To have Carmen speak to your group, please visit **http://www.thetwentythirdpsalm.com**

Thank you to those who graciously
shared your single-parent triumphs and trials.
Your stories give others hope.